AVIGNON

Avignon seen from the right bank of the Rhone. Lithography by R. Bonnard - 1700 (Calvet Museum)

AVIGNON - ITS HISTORY

ORIGINS:

A natural refuge, easy to protect, located at the confluence of the Rhône and the Durance rivers, the rock of Avignon has been inhabited since earliest times. Archeological research has shown traces of human presence as early as the Neolithic Age.

It is said that the people of Cavari gave their town the name of Aouenion, from Celtic or Ligurian words meaning for some "town of violent wind" or "lord of the waters" for others. Whichever, the image is in both cases extremely vivid.

GREEK PERIOD:

When the Phoenicians founded Marseille in the year 600 B.C., they also showed interest in the city of Aouenion, wonderfully situated for commercial exchanges, and build a large river port there. However, Aouenion maintained its independence and issued its own currency, based on the Massalian model.

ROMAN PERIOD:

In the year 49 B.C., Julius Caesar, after the siege of Marseilles, captured the city of Aouenion from the Marseillais. This is the period when the Romans organize "Gallia Narbonensis" in which Avignon becomes one of the most important towns. During the Roman period, the port built by the Massaliots was extensively used. The town then took the name of Avenio.

- Under Augustus, the town formed part of the eighty cities of Gaul.

- Under Claudius, it received the title of Latin Colony.
- Under Hadrian, it became a Roman City. But this widespread honourific title had lost some of its significance and Arles, Orange and Nîmes were similarly honoured at the start of Roman colonization. Gallo-Roman Avignon covered an area estimated at 6 hectares and had approximately 27,000 inhabitants.

THE BARBARIAN INVASIONS - THE MIDDLE AGES

Thanks to its strong fortifications erected by the Romans and to its strategic position, Avignon withstood the Vandal and Goth invasions. But in 474, the Burgundians finally overcame its resistance, to be followed by the Wisigoths and finally the Goths. In the 8C, the Arabs invaded Provence and Avignon became one of their strongholds. In 737, Charles Martel freed the city after an historic and bloody siege. Present Rue Rouge or "Red Street" is said to owe its name to this terrible period due to the human blood which ran down it in torrents. But, violent as this siege was, Charles Martel had to take this much-coveted town a second time, from the Saracens.

There followed a period when Avignon successively belonged to the Holy Roman Empire of Charlemagne, the kingdom of Aquitaine, and finally to Provence, which was raised to the state of kingdom in 879 under King Boson. The kingdom of Provence was finally extended to the whole of the Rhône basin, as far as the Mediterranean.

In 932, Avignon came into the possession of the kingdom of Arles, which was incorporated in the Holy Roman Empire in 1033.

In the final period of the Middle Ages, Avignon was a possession of the Count of Provence. This was the source of much fratricidal dispute and ended in the division of the city between the counts of Toulouse and Forcalquier in 1125.

The title of Count of Avignon was hereditary and was generally attributed to the Boson family.

In 1129, Avignon was raised to the state of free town. Liberated from the authority of the Counts, the town was administered by elected magistrates or podestas.

This period was beneficial for Avignon which became a prosperous town and commercial centre where the middle classes were richer and free from feodal obligations. In 1154, Bishop Geoffrey drew up the Consulate Charter (bylaws). The bishops and archbishops often helped to free towns and this was particularly true for Avignon. Its method of government, through podestas and a council, meant that no taxes were levied on the population of Avignon.

In 1226, a confident Avignon denied passage to Louis VIII, King of France on his way to wage war against the Albigensians. The royal army laid siege to the town which surrended after three months, overcome by famine.

The ramparts were demolished and Saint Bénézet bridge seriously damaged. After this surrender, Avignon retained only the shadow of its former freedom. However, it did keep the right to elect its podestas, but on condition that the bishop approved the choice. Abolition of the free town status was ratified by the convention of Baucaire (headquarters of the Princes) on May 7th 1251.

In 1290, Charles II of Anjou became master of Avignon.

In 1303, the law school, founded by the Counts of Provence, wasraised to University status by Pope Boniface VIII.

The University, famous for the quality of its professors, attracted many foreigners for its science teaching.

AVIGNON BECAME THE CAPITAL OF THE CHRISTIAN WORLD

For almost one hundred years, the city lived in prosperity and refinement. Thanks to the fame of its university, it was a town of sciences which attracted the greatest minds of the century. The sovereign pontiffs chose Avignon as the papal city for political and geographical reasons during this century.

Rome was politically unstable at the time whereas Avignon offered peaceful serenity.

Charles of Anjou, Count of Provence, sole master of Avignon, had always been a faithful vassal of the church.

The town of Avignon was also favourably situated for international relation being at the confluence of the Rhône and Durance valleys, important lines of communication at the time.

The Papal Palace with the new Palace in the foreground and the Basilica Notre-Dame des Doms.

THE SEVEN POPES OF AVIGNON

JOHN XXII

Two years' later, the cardinals finally gathered in the convent of the Dominican order of friars in Lyons. It took them six months to agree but finally, on August 7th, 1316, Jacques Duèse, Cardinal of Porto, 72 years old, was elected Pope John XXII. The new Pope settled into the episcopal palace in Avignon in which he had been a bishop from 1310 until 1313. His great age suggested that his pontificate would be very short, but it finally lasted 18 years. An excellent administrator, at his death he left the church great wealth.

CLEMENT VI

Clement VI was a famous orator and theologian, and, in contrast to his predecessor, an ostentatious lord. He was elected in 1342. A patron of the arts, he attracted a great number of artists, wise men and scholars to the court, in particular the great poet and humanist Petrarch, who was to become his ambassador. The important Avignon school of painting was born from the coming together of many Italian painters. Clement VI bought Avignon from Queen Joan for 80,000 gold florins. The magnificence of this pontificate was tarnished by aterrible plague which began the persecution of the Jews, to whom the Pope offered his protection. He died in 1352.

CLEMENT V

The first pontiff of the Provençal city, elected in Perouse and crowned in the presence of King Philip the Fair in Lyons in 1305. He settled in Avignon four years later in 1309, and lived in the Dominican convent, rue Annonelle.

Although he caused no great upheavels in the life of the city, he did establish the papacy for a century to come.

He died in 1314 after having worked towards a "rapprochement" between the kings of France and England for a new crusade.

BENOIT XII

Jacques Fourrier was elected Pope Benoît XII by the first conclave held in Avignon of December 20th, 1334.

Born a baker's son in the earldom on Foix, he continued to wear the white robes of the Cistercian Order from which he came. During his austere reign, Benoît XII fought against the excesses of the Church and reminded the religious orders of their original rules. A man of peace, he tried to calm the rising dissensions within the Italian church. He had a more spacious building erected with stronger fortifications to replace the old episcopal palace. He died in 1342.

INNOCENT VI

Elected in 1352, Etienne Aubert was a jurist renowned for his honesty. The reign of Innocent VI resembled that of Benoît XII. He broke away from the high living of Clement VI and increased the Church's wealth. He finished the work on the pontifical palace and built new city walls. He died in 1362.

URBAN V

Guillaume of Grimoard was elected Pope on September 22nd, 1362, after much controversy.

At the time, he was the priest of Saint Victor Church in Marseilles to which he remained particularly attached. He took the name of Urban V.

During his reign, he tried unsuccessfully to reestablish the pontificate in Rome. Indeed, according to him, the Pope was in exile in Avignon. While Pope, he went on wearing the simple robes of the Benedictine order of monks and followed their austere rules.

His reign, marked by his good sense and kindness and praised by Petrarch himself, lasted only eight years.

GREGOIRE XI

Elected in 1370, he fulfilled the wish of Urban V to return the pontificate to Rome.

On his death in 1378, an Italian, Urban VI, was elected the new Pope.

The end of Gregory XI's reign marked the beginning of the Great Schism. It is a period of much disturbance and tension for the Catholic Church which was divided into two clans supporting Rome and Avignon respectively. This division ended at the Council of Constance (1414-1418) with the acknowledgement of Martin V as the one and only Pope of the Catholic Church.

Avignon lost its title of capital of Christendom. But throughout this century, the City of the Popes grew, was embellished, fortified and repopulated (30,000 inhabitants). Many new churches were built to replace the decrepit Roman buildings.

View of Avignon from Bartelasse Island. 19C lithography.

THE AGE OF LEGATES -15C AND 16C

For about two centuries, Avignon was governed by Legates appointed by the Pope. The first of these Legates, Pierre de Foix, governed the town with serene sagacity. This was a prosperous period for the city when the university flourished and arts developed. Many artists were attracted to Avignon from all horizons, and contributed to its embellishment.

During the Renaissance, the Italian inspiration, which had been somewhat forgotten during the Great Schism, made a strong come back. François Ist stayed in the city and used it as a camp in September 1536 during the second invasion of Provence by Charles-Quint.

Avignon was visited by many sovereigns, but the most sumptuous reception was the one given to Louis XIV who was to marry the infant Maria Theresa of Spain, daughter of King Philip IV. The town's magistrates gave the sovereign 200 gold medals bearing his effigy.

Sand was spread on the streets of Avignon and the houses decorated with tapistries. For his departure, Saint Bénézet bridge was draped in scarlet velvet.

17TH CENTURY

In 1653, Avignon went through a period of internal violence, "the Avignon insurrection", which opposed the Pessugaux (nobles of the town) and the Pevoulins (from the poorer classes). In 1693, Avignon was no longer administered by Legates but by vice-legates under the authority of Rome.

The town lost all political control, but nevertheless lived a period of relative calm. Teaching, art, literature and music developed thanks to its cosmopolitan population.

THE FRENCH REVOLUTION

During the French Revolution, the population revolted, the Consulate was overthrown and replaced by a municipal authority which adopted the national colours. On May 25th, 1791, Avignon was incorporated into the French nation along with the earldom of Venaissin. This incorporation led to great changes for the population; the madder and silk industries developed and many convents were converted into workshops or lodgings to meet the needs of the growing population (80,000 at the end of the 18C).

1854

The poets Mistral, Aubanel, Mathieu, Roumanille, Tavan, Giera and Brunet founded the literary movement, "Le Félibrige". Today, Avignon has become a modern city which remembers its prestigious history and still constitutes a large cultural and artistic centre.

This aerial view of Doms Rock with St Bénézet Bridge in the foreground offers a general view of "the most beautiful and the strongest house in the World" (Froissart): the Papal Palace.

THE PAPAL PALACE

"The most beautiful and strongest house in the world" according to Froissart, a 14C poet and chronicler.

Pope Benoît XII was the first to begin construction of the pontifical palace, with Pierre Poisson as master-builder. This first part of the building is called the "Old Palace".

A Romanesque style fortress and palace, it reflects the austerity which marked the reign of the third pontiff in the capital of Christendom.

His successor, Clement VI, patron of the arts and letters and a great-hearted man, wished for a palace closer to his tastes for art and luxury. So he ordered the construction of the "New Palace", in a lighter style of Gothic architecture.

The master-builder, Jean de Loubière, was also French, whereas an Italian, Matteo Giovannetti, was entrusted with the pictorial decoration. This painter was to continue his work under the reign of Clement VI's successor and became known as "the Pope's painter". Innocent VI completed the monumental master-piece by adding two towers (Saint Laurent Tower and Gâche Tower) and fortifying the great chapel. In 1518, Cardinal François de Clermont-Lodève had a new room built in the palace gardens, "la Mirande".

The vice-legates could not afford to maintain this sumptuous building and it gradually fell into disrepair.

Under the Revolution, the pontifical palace was used as a prison and greatly damaged.

Under the Consulate, it was turned into barracks until 1906, when it was entrusted to the Department of Historical Monuments for restoration.

Enter the palace through the Champeaux Gate or the Saint Peter and Paul Gate topped by the spires of the two towers and ornated with shields bearing the coat of arms of Pope Clement VI. The pentagonal tower is to be admired at the corner of the façade.

The colossal whole of this monument: the Basilica Notre-Dame des Doms and Campane Tower, part of the Palace where Jean XXII set up court when he arrived in Avignon in 1316. The different Popes transformed and enlarged it to create the Papal Palace.

The more ornate facade of the new Palace. In the centre is the "Great Dignatories wing" and Champeaux door set on its fortified towers. On the left is Gache Tower. On the extreme right is the western wall of the Great Audience Chamber and the Great Chapel (the local figure Jean de Loubière was work co-ordinator)

The new Palace. Champeaux door, from the name of the street leading up to it, framed by the two fortified towers which were ▶ restored in 1933 and surmounted with the arms of Pope Clement VI

The two parts of the Palace are clearly distinct. On the left is the facade of the old Benoit XII palace, set back, fortified and austere with Campale tower. On the right is the new Palace (Clement VI)

SAINT JOHN'S CHAPEL

This is also called the Consistory Chapel since it adjoins the Consistory room. It is decorated with frescoes attributed to Matteo Giovannetti, representing scenes from the life of Saint John the Baptist and Saint John the Apostle.

Saint John's Chapel: the west wall dedicated to Saint John the Apostle. Upper vault: on the right is Saint John the Apostle; on the left, Mary Salome, mother of Saint John the Apostle. Upper register: the crucifixion showing the recommendation of the Virgin Mary to Saint John. Lower register: on the left, the martyrdom of Saint John, immersion in boiling oil, close to the latin door. On the right, the disappearance of Saint John in the grave he had dug at the foot of the altar.

Saint John's Chapel: the north wall dedicated to Saint John the Baptist. Upper vault: in the centre, God the Father, the dove of peace and Christ in prayer; on the left, the baptism of Christ by Saint John; on the right, Saint John questioned by the priests and the levites. Lower register: Herod's feast at which the executioner presents the head of Saint John, beheaded in Herod's dungeons to satisfy the vengeance of Herodias.

THE CONSISTORY

This is a large room measuring 34 metres long by 10.50 metres wide where the Pope met with his cardinals in great ceremony. The walls were formerly covered with frescoes by Giovannetti, including a scene depicting the crowning of the Virgin Lady in the presence of four Popes. These frescoes were destroyed during a fire in 1413. At present, contemporary portraits of the various Popes of Avignon and Gobelin tapestries decorate this room which, throughout the 14C, was the scene of the most important events in the political and religious life of the pontifical city. Two doors give into this room, one of which was reserved for the Pope.

Saint John's Chapel: the south wall dedicated to Saint John the Apostle. Upper vault in two parts: on the left, Saint Anne, maternal grandmother of Saint John the Apostle; on the right, Zebede, the father of Saint John. Upper register: Zebede and his two sons fishing from their boat; John and James rowing. Lower register: on the left, the vision of Saint John at Patmos, apparition of Christ holding a double-pointed sword, behind him the seven golden candlesticks (from the Apocalypse); on the right, the resurrection of Drusania by Saint John at Ephesus (from the Lives of the Saints).

THE KITCHENS

Several rooms on three levels, make up the kitchens: stores, cellars, and bottling and pantler's office where the wine and bread were prepared. Many people were occupied in purchasing and storing supplies, and banquets were frequently held there. The high kitchen still retains its remarkable vault and its octogonal pyramid-shaped chimney.

THE GRAND TINEL

Named after the latin word "tina", once meaning dining room, it is the largest room in the palace at 48 metres long.

The vault is now panelled, but originally Matteo Giovannetti decorated it with gold spangled stars on an azure blue background. This hall was devastated by a fire in 1413.

On ceremonial occasions and banquets, the meals of the Pope and guests were served in this hall. The walls were draped with gold and silver hangings, the menus were Gargantuan, with entertainment by jugglers, troubadours, dancing and tournaments.

SAINT MARTIAL'S CHAPEL

Used by the cardinals for deliberations and voting, this small oratory is situated above Saint John's Chapel and adjoins the Grand Tinel. The frescoes by Matteo Giovannetti magnificently illustrate the life of Saint Martial of Limoges. According to legend, he was a contemporary of Christ who came to christianize Gaul. He carried a staff given to him by Saint Peter with which he is said to have resuscitated the dead.

Vault of Saint Martial's Chapel: North side: christianization of the Gauls, Saint Martial ordains Saint Aurelien and consecrates the thirteen churches founded by the Saint.
West side: the miracle of Agen, Saint Martial forces the Devil out of the statue of Jupiter, healing of a paralytic man.
South side: the miracle of Tulle, deliverance of a possessed person, resurrection of the son of the Lord of Tulle.
East side: death of Saint Martial, his soul borne away by two angels.

Saint Martial's chapel. West wall: upper chapter: miracle of the holy staff; left to right: destruction of the idols by Duke Etienne, healing of the paralyzed Count of Bordeaux by touching the staff; the fire of Bordeaux extinguished by the holy staff; lower chapter: martyrdom of Saint Peter and Saint Paul, announced to Saint Martial by Christ; Saint Martial's vision.

ROBING ROOM

This is also called the state room and formed the pontifical antechamber. It is situated between the Grand Tinel and the papal bedchamber. It was partly destroyed in the 19C. Visitors who obtained a private audience had to wait here. The Pope gave audiences either in his study, in his bedchamber or else in his robing room where the "cathedra", a canopied throne adorned with gold drapes, would be placed.

PAPAL BEDCHAMBER

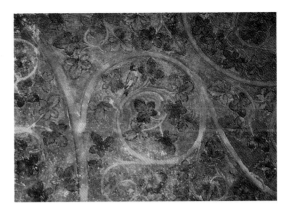

The papal bedchamber is in the sturdy monumental Popes' tower, also called the Treasure Tower. This square room is gaily decorated with wall paintings showing many birds and squirrels in foliage. The present stained glass windows bearing the arms of John XXII are only reproductions of the originals. Apart from the Pope, the modestly ranked chamberlains, in the Pope's personal service, also slept in this room.

THE STAG ROOM

In 1342, Clement VI had the Wardrobe Tower built, with a bath-house, two tiers of wardrobes and, close to the Papal Bedchamber, a kind of living-room or study richly decorated with secular subjects from country life and hunting scenes. These frescoes date back to 1344 but the artist is unknown.

On the left is a deer hunting scene; in the centre is a fishing scene; on the right is an apple harvesting scene.
Bottom left: *Wall decoration: falcon hunting (detail)*

THE GREAT AUDIENCE CHAMBER

Built by Jean de Loubière, this great hall measures 52 m by 15.80 m and is divided down its centre into two naves with vaulted ceiling supported by five columns. It was used as the law court for the Rote court, formed of thirteen ecclesiastical judges.

Part of a ceiling fresco by Mateo Giovannetti representing the prophets

THE GREAT CHAPEL OF CLEMENT VI

Formerly called the "new chapel", this vast chapel measures 52 m long and 19.50 m high and was built in the purest southern Gothic style.

Effigy of Benoit XII (casting)

The Great Chapel door ▶

Bottom left - *Small Audience Chamber: detail of vaults and ceiling decoration*

On leaving the Consistory, the serenity of Benoit XII cloister

SAINT BENEZET BRIDGE

Constructed in the 17C, this, the famous "Pont d'Avignon", originally had 22 arches and measured 900 metres long. During the siege of Avignon, Louis VIII ordered it to be almost completely destroyed. Reconstruction work was carried out until the 17C but the unpredictability of the Rhône caused much damage to this impressive civil engineering feat.

Despite the goodwill of the people of Avignon during this century, only four arches of the bridge and Saint Nicholas' Chapel still stand. Built on two storeys, the chapel as the burial place of Benezet, shepherd of Provence, who, according to the legend, built the bridge. In 1674, the remains of the Saint were taken to Celestins' Church from which they disappeared during the French Revolution.

METROPOLITAN BASILICA, NOTRE-DAME DES DOMS, CATHEDRAL OF AVIGNON

Cathedral of the diocese of Avignon, the basilica acquired its Metropolitan title more than five centuries ago, when Avignon was raised to the rank of archbishopric by Pope Sixte IV.

A basilica is thought to have been built on the site as early as the 4C. The present building dates back to the second half of the 12C and was transformed during the l5C and 17C.

The square belfry, which collapsed in 1405, was rebuilt in 1425. The apse was destroyed in 1672 to be replaced by a much larger building. A Baroque tribune was also added to the pure Romanesque style nave along the side walls.

During the Revolution, Notre-Dame des Doms was abandoned and damaged. It was handed back for services only in 1822, after restoration by the archbishop. The imposing gilded cast-iron statue of the Blessed Virgin was installed on the belfry in 1859.

Notre Dame des Doms. The statue of the immaculate Virgin erected in 1859 crowns the bell tower

The inside: the Romanesque nave, the 12C tribune in the background, the chancel and the 12C master altar

Painted stone Christ dating from the 16 century

The tomb of Benoit VII

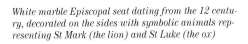

White marble Episcopal seat dating from the 12 century, decorated on the sides with symbolic animals representing St Mark (the lion) and St Luke (the ox)

THE TOMB OF POPE JEAN XXII

The tomb was moved from its original location in 1759 to improve passage. It was arranged so that the head faced the rising sun, eternal symbol of the expected return of Christ.

Severely damaged during the Revolution, when the Pope's body was profaned and thrown into the Rhone, this magnificent, highly decorated, baldachin tomb is in a style which is similar to the tombs found in many English churches. This suggests that it was designed and executed by an English artist Hugues Wilfred, architect of the Treasure Chapel. However, others attribute it to Jean Lavenier.

There is no longer a body in the tomb, the body of Pope John XXII having been broken and the bones scattered during the Revolution.

LE PETIT PALAIS (Small palace)

Built at the foot of the Doms hill in 1327 for Arnaud de Via, nephew of Pope John XXII, this palace owes its name to its smaller size compared to the pontifical palace.

In 1336, Benoît XII purchased it and gave it to the Bishop of Avignon. In 1364, Urban V made it the permanent "livery of the Bishop of Avignon" and it is in this more modest pontifical palace that he chose to die.

The small palace was fortified during the Great Schism.

In the 15C, the cardinals Alain de Coëtivy and his successor Julien de la Rovère had it reconstructed and modernized, decorating it more in the style of the period.

The small palace housed many prestigious visitors, including César Borgia in 1493, François 1st in 1533, Anne of Austria and the Duke of Orleans in 1663.

It now houses some beautiful collections from the Avignon School between the 12C and 16C, taken from Calvet Museum.

Virgin and child by Botticelli from the end of the 15 century

Top: *the Small Palace, 15C facade. It houses a museum very rich in contemporary works of the history of the Popes. In the background is St Benezet Bridge and Fort André de Villeneuve les Avignon in the distance.*

Left: *The Calvary by Ludovico Urbani, a work of violent impressionism and exceptional quality (Petit Palace Museum).*

Right: *Central part of the retable of the San Francisco Convent Chapel in Savona by G. Massone, 15 century.*

Bottom: *First of four panels by the master Cassoni Campana. Mythological history of the loves of Pasiphaé, birth of the Minotaur.*

The Papal Palace with vice-legate procession by CL Gordot 1722-1804 (Calvet Museum)

PLACE DU PALAIS (Palace square)

In 1404, Pope Benoît XIII (1394-1409, during the Great Schism), had some of the houses pulled down in order to clear the bottom of the Papal Palace walls.

This was to avoid any concealed approach to the Palace.

The result is grandiose. This immense space, lined by the most magnificent monuments in the city, is considered one of the most beautiful squares in the world. It was here that the guillotine played its sombre role in the Terror from March to June 1794.

In contrast, modern-day artists erect their easels here during the Festival of Avignon which enlivens the old City of the Popes every year in July.

THE OLD MINT (Hôtel des Monnaies)

Facing the Papal Palace, the Old Mint which was built in 1619 is the most Italian-inspired building in Avignon in an exuberant Baroque style. The eagles and dragons decorating its façade are from the coat of arms of Pope Paul V.

Since 1860, the Old Mint has housed the Avignon School of Music.

PLACE DE L'HORLOGE (Clock Tower Square)

This site was already the Roman Forum of the ancient city and vital centre of the town in which it became the largest market. There are traces of the tower constructed by Bishop Ardoint Aubert, nephew of Pope Innocent VI in 1363. In 1447, the town associations bought it together with the adjoining buildings to set up the Common House, which they rented to the Benedictines of Saint Laurent. In 1458, the square was enlarged and became known as the Common House Grounds.

It finally took on its modern name of Place de~l'Horloge in 1471 when the town installed a clock on top of the tower. Two automatons called Jacquemarts ring out the hours.

The theatre which was rebuilt in 1846. The monument is well balanced and elegant. On either side of the entrance are statues to Corneille and Moliere

Calvet Museum. The frontage and the park of the hotel Villeneuve Martignan (17 century)

Saint Michel. Germany, 15 century. Multicolour wood, 1.30 m high (Calvet Museum)

CALVET MUSEUM, MANSION VILLENEUVE MARTIGNAN

This is one of the most sumptuous mansions in Avignon, built in 1742 by Jean Baptiste and François Franque. The sculptures are the work of Pierre Bondon. Purchased by the town in 1833, it shelters Calvet Museum, named after the generous donor Esprit Claude François Calvet, doctor, archeologist, numismatist and bibliophile.

Deceased in 1810, he left the town of Avignon his library, his artistic treasures and money needed to set up the museum. Since then other donors have enriched its possessions, particularly Esprit Requien and the family Jouve of Cavaillon.

"Midi sur terre, coup de vent" by Vernet Claude 1714-1789 (Calvet Museum)

Fire, one of the four elements by Jean Breughel 1568 -1625 (Calvet Museum)

The death of Bara by David (Calvet Museum)

SAINT PETER'S CHURCH

In 1358, Cardinal Pierre de Prado had this church rebuilt. The work was unfinished until the 16C. The remarkable façade, of flamboyant Gothic style, also bears some elements of the Renaissance style. But it is mainly its gate, one of the most beautiful in Provence, which commands admiration. Its massive doors cut from hard walnut trees were carved by Antoine Volard in 1551.

DOMS GARDENS

Emperor Augustus wanted to build a temple dedicated to the north wind on this gigantic barren rock. Over the years, the antique city gradually expanded at the foot of the rock and, since the 17C, the gardens have become a favourite promenade. Sumptuously arranged, decorated with statues and embellished by small lakes, it is very pleasant to stroll round. It offers dazzling views over the Rhone, the Benezet bridge and, in the distance, Mount Ventoux.

There is a train for tourists trips around the gardens.

SAINT AGRICOL CHURCH

Of a later date than the cathedral, but certainly the oldest church in Avignon, Saint Agricol church is thought to bear the name of its founder, the bishop of Avignon, in the 12C.

During the second half of the 15C, Saint Agricol church was greatly modified, enlarged, embellished and given a new façade, characteristic of the Provençal style of the period. A beautiful Blessed Virgin and Child, assumed to be the work of wood carver Ferrier Bernard, tempts us across the threshold of the carved wooden doors.

THE RAMPARTS OF THE PAPAL CITY

One of the undeniable charms of Avignon is certainly the vast city walls which encircle it. Stendhal praised their autumn leaf colour, bright under the Provençal sun. These ramparts, which were built between 1352 and 1370, originally had twelve city gates. Only four still remain.

Generations of master-builders were involved in erecting this civil engineering structure which has been a constant work site throughout the history of Avignon.

In 1846, an engineer called Talabot suggested that the railway could be installed along the walls with a station. Prosper Mérimée strongly protested against this project which he called a "public misfortune" in a report to the Ministry. Fortunately the project was abandoned.

The ramparts were restored by Viollet-le-Duc in the second half of the 19C.

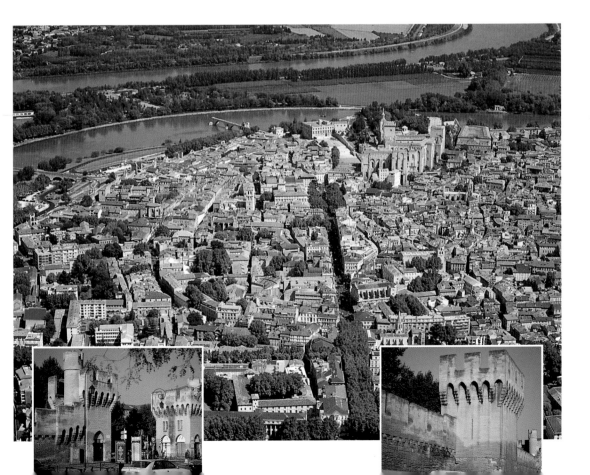

VILLENEUVE-LES-AVIGNON

Facing the ancient City of the Popes, on the right bank of the Rhône, nestling at the foot of Fort Saint Andre, is Villeneuve-les-Avignon. The origins of this small town are to be found in a cave in Mount Andaon, where, in the 5C, Saint Casarie chose to retire and finish his days as a hermit.

The Benedictine monastery of Saint André was founded here in the 10C. Quickly prospering, and possessing large estates, it became the "Saint André Abbey" and a small medieval town grew up nearby. Until the 13C, the small town lived under the domination of its powerful neighbour Avignon. But in 1226, Saint André Abbey freed itself and concluded a treaty of protection with King Louis VIII, a feudal arrangement which tied it to the King of France.

After this treaty was renewed by King Philip the

Innocent VI's mausoleum

Fair in 1292, the population grew and a new town was built with straight streets radiating out from a central square.

PHILIP THE FAIR'S TOWER

Philip the Fair's Tower was built between 1293 and 1307 at the entrance of Saint Benezet bridge, opposite the defensive Tower of Avignon. There was also a fortified building of which nothing remains today.

At the time, a ground floor and one upper floor were built, with a second floor added in the 14C.

A climb to the lookout post offers splendid views over the river and the city of the Popes. Villeneuve reached the peak of its prestige when the Popes made Avignon their capital. Many residences, small palaces and liveries were built to house the Church officials that Avignon, overpopulated, could not accomodate.

The magnificence of the pontifical court overflowed into Villeneuve-les-Avignon. When the Popes left, the small city went through a more modest period, but still remained important. The 17C and 18C brought considerable architectural and artistic revival. The revolution saw much destruction, but, fortunately, the 20C has brought much restoration to the city whose history is closely connected with that of the City of the Popes.

FORT SAINT ANDRE

A military post capping Mount Andaon, Fort Saint Andre sheltered, among others, the small chapel of Notre Dame de Belvezet and Saint Andre Abbey. The fort walls are more elaborate than the contemporary ramparts of Avignon. The city walls were built after the treaty of protection between Saint Andre Abbey and King John the Good of France, which was signed in 1362. The crenal-topped walls have only one access door, flanked by twin towers.

The visitor can admire the surrounding countryside from the battlements.

CARTHUSIAN MONASTERY OF VAL-DE-BENE-DICTION

The Carthusian monastery of Villeneuve was founded in remembrance of the gesture of humility by Jean Birel from the Carthusian order of monks who, after having been appointed by the conclave on December 6th, 1352 to succeed Clement VI, refused to become Pope in order to stay a humble servant of God.

Elected in his stead, Innocent VI founded this Carthusian monastery in 1356 and, according to his wish, it became his burial place in 1362. His family continued enlarging and embellishing the monastery. The revolution caused severe damage but its restoration has been actively pursued throughout the 20C.

Saint Andrew Fort (14 century)

From St Andrew's Fort, a series of small houses wonderfully preserved lead to the foot of Philip the Good Tower

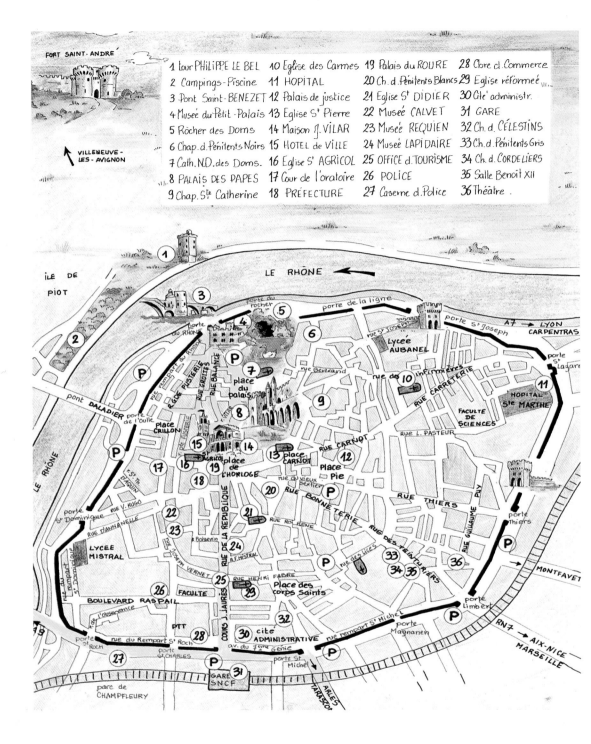

FORT SAINT-ANDRÉ

VILLENEUVE - LES-AVIGNON

1 tour PHILIPPE LE BEL
2 Campings-Piscine
3 Pont Saint-BENEZET
4 Musée du Petit-Palais
5 Rocher des Doms
6 Chap. d. Pénitents Noirs
7 Cath. N.D. des Doms.
8 PALAIS DES PAPES
9 Chap. Ste Catherine
10 Eglise des Carmes
11 HOPITAL
12 Palais de justice
13 Eglise St Pierre
14 Maison J. VILAR
15 HOTEL de VILLE
16 Eglise St AGRICOL
17 Cour de l'oratoire
18 PRÉFECTURE
19 Palais du ROURE
20 Ch. d. Pénitents Blancs
21 Eglise St DIDIER
22 Musée CALVET
23 Musée REQUIEN
24 Musée LAPIDAIRE
25 OFFICE d. TOURISME
26 POLICE
27 Caserne d. Police
28 Cbre d. Commerce
29 Eglise réformée
30 Cité administr.
31 GARE
32 Ch. d. CÉLESTINS
33 Ch. d. Pénitents Gris
34 Ch. d. CORDELIERS
35 Salle Benoît XII
36 Théâtre.

Text: Roselyne Moreaux
Artwork: Agnès Gojan
Photo: Ph. Caudron - H. Chappe
Réalisation: Sté. PEC
Direction: 1er semestre 1998

Editions PEC - 13240 Septèmes les Vallons
ZAC de la Haute Bedoule - Quartier Actimart - Ilot D
Tél: 04.91.65.32.76 - Fax: 04.91.65.32.79
ISBN 2-84293-056-8 / ISSN 1275-5141
Printed in U.E.